Meditations of John Burroughs

CHRIS HIGHLAND

MEDITATIONS OF JOHN BURROUGHS

NATURE IS HOME

2007

Meditations of John Burroughs

CONTENTS

"The whole gospel of my books
(if they have any gospel) is
'Stay at home; see the wonderful and the beautiful
in the simple things all about you; make the most
of the common and the near at hand.'
When I have gone abroad, I have carried this spirit
with me, and have tested what I have seen
by the nature revealed to me at my own doorstep."

~John Burroughs, letter to Clara Barrus (1909)
{*Our Friend John Burroughs,* Clara Barrus, 1914}

To My Nieces And Nephews
Isaac, Jessica,
Hannah, Zachary And Nathan

INTRODUCTION

*"I shall not be imprisoned in that grave where you are to bury my
body. I shall be diffused in great Nature, in the soil, in the air, in
the sunshine, in the hearts of those who love me, in all the living
and flowing currents of the world.... { I } go back into this vast,
wonderful, divine cosmos."*
~John Burroughs

***

In the month of April one year before the birth of John Muir
in Scotland, a child was born in the Catskill Mountains of
New York who, like Muir, would grow to love the lessons
of Nature and sing the praises of Nature to inspire generations.
His name was John Burroughs (1837-1921). Maybe it was
fitting that this influential naturalist would die, in his eighty-
third year, on a train returning to his East Coast home from
California on the West. He was a man who spanned distances in
life and in death. Friend of Muir, he also became a companion
to Theodore Roosevelt, Thomas Edison and Henry Ford. His
writing delighted everyone from schoolchildren to the Queen of
England. His books on Nature, numbering nearly thirty from
1867 to his death in 1921, covered birds and mammals, trees,
seasons, botany, philosophy, religion, camping with Roosevelt
and much more.

Given his family history one might wonder how it came
about that John Burroughs was an adventuring naturalist on

the open fields of ideas. He emerged from a pioneering stock of farmers with plows digging all the way back to his great-great grandparents. His grandfather Eden cleared land and built a log house in the backwoods near Roxbury, New York about 1795. Eden was a sweat-of-the-brow Baptist whose bible was always close at hand. John Burroughs' father, Chauncey (b. 1803) was also a pure-bred Baptist who only read the bible and religious literature, never said "Thank You" in his life, and "was quite unconscious of the beauties of nature" (*Our Friend John Burroughs*). One of Chauncey Burroughs' greatest fears was that his son John, who showed such a love for books, would become a Methodist minister. His mother Amy (b. 1808) was the tenth child in her Irish family and had ten children of her own. Though uneducated, she worked harder on the farm than anyone, was a brooding Baptist and, because she was not interested in reading, never read any of her son's books. Apart from the religious zeal of immediate family, there were several well-educated, ordained clergy in the Burroughs clan. In 1692 The Rev. George Burroughs, a Harvard graduate, was, for some reason, hanged during the witch trials in Salem. A cousin of John Burroughs' father, The Rev. John C. Burroughs graduated from Yale and became the first president of Chicago University. Stephen Burroughs was "a renegade preacher" in the 1700s and there were other relatives who became preachers in the next century. Perhaps with this rich and fertile field as his background it may not appear quite as strange that John Burroughs the Nature writer would be grounded in soil as well as religion. The sage of Slabsides (the rustic cabin he built in the woods of upstate New York) revealed an intimacy with Nature and the great questions that arise from that intimate relation—a delighted curiosity that often tills the seedbeds of heretical religion.

Burroughs did not avoid the trail of controversy. He sparred with Muir, critiqued other writers such as Emerson, Thoreau, William Long and Ernest Thompson Seton, and he audaciously rattled the orthodoxy of his day by not just publishing a book on Walt Whitman but lauding him as "the greatest incarnation of mind, heart and soul"—"the Poet of the Cosmos" (*Accepting the Universe—AU*). Later in life his works on religion, which he respected as "spiritual attraction," a feeling of "the mystery and spirituality of the universe," took on an almost prophetic tone. It was clear to Burroughs: religion was waning, declining before the light of reason, of science and natural philosophy.

It is exactly this rich composting of spirituality and nature that attracts the attention of contemporary readers. We are enticed by Burroughs' somewhat novel *naturalistic philosophy*. He presents us with his own migrations, peregrinations really, across verdant lands usually left to professional philosophers and theologians (he once said that the most valuable elements of his books, primarily the feeling and love he expressed in them, came from his mother Amy and it was her side of the family—the Kellys—whose "meditative kind" of religion was the proper balance for the intellectual depth of his father's side). Burroughs brings his experienced scientific senses into a deep dialogue with explorers of ideas. With his naturalist's eye wide open, he treks about the great questions of life and the universe, drawing us into the migratory current, the tidal flow of all things, toward an acceptance of the cosmos and an emergence from the dark, ignorant past into an illuminated present (hence his books *Accepting the Universe* and *The Light of Day*). Through his natural sermons, delivered from the rough-hewn pulpit carved with his own pioneer-and-preacher ancestry, he offers us a fundamentally positive hopefulness—a spirituality we can homestead, in the great house of the universe.

The natural world presented Burroughs with a perpetual tide of ideas. For him, Nature was a vast classroom of wonder displaying lessons for the scientist and for the philosopher. In *Field and Study* (1919) he wrote, "To find an interest in natural history one must add something more than the fact, one must see the meaning of the fact." The only way to discover this meaning is to leap into the woodsy classroom. "The wild life around one becomes interesting the moment one gets into the current of it…" (FS). Significantly, this naturalist launched his scientific mind deep enough into that current to be carried along into the wilds of spiritual thought as well.

Burroughs is both intriguing and disturbing in his dismantling of modern religion. He is equally radical in the organic, living, breathing replacement for the old theologies. His perceptive scientific mind pushed him to take on the most sensitive issues of faith. Yet Burroughs had no interest in founding some new religion. He said that one who attempted that would just as well get crucified. While he understood that the masses of people "are not yet prepared for a religion based upon natural knowledge alone" he was confident that "the time is surely coming" (*The Light of Day*—LD).

What Burroughs recognized and passionately urged us toward (echoing Thoreau, Emerson, Fuller, Whitman, Muir and others) was an *open air religious sense* driven by reason, science and an enlightened *divine ideal*. For us to grow up and be healthier as a human community we must, in Burroughs' mind, abandon the God of the Puritans, and Calvinism in particular—a deity who was "a monster too terrible to contemplate" (LD). Burroughs was pleased that even in his time, large numbers of people were coming to understand that "the earth is divine, and that God is everywhere" (FS). Of course, what Burroughs meant by "God" sets the context for the whole discussion.

The writings of this spiritual fieldguide direct the reader to a serious rethinking of divinity. That which is divine or sacred, must begin and end with the Cosmos. For Burroughs the seminal question becomes "Is there an outside to the Cosmos, a beyond?" (FS). His response is as open as the blue sky, as far-reaching as the Hubble telescope: "We accept Nature as we find it, and do not crave the intervention of a God that sits behind and is superior to it" (AU). There is no one who "sits apart from Nature" to rule, judge or determine anything. Ultimately this means, "When we see [humanity] as a part of Nature, we see [humanity] as a part of God" (AU). There is no beyond, no Other, no outside. There is only what is, and we call this Nature, Cosmos, the Universe, and sometimes we name it God.

To call this collection from a cross-section of Burroughs' work "meditations" might make old John smile. Truth is, these represent *my* meditations on Burroughs' "spiritual side." The irony is, he believed as well as I, that spirit and matter are not exclusive nor are they anything but identical. It is as much science as it is spirituality to say, "We are all made of one stuff... vegetable and animal, man and woman, dog and donkey" and the secret to this is "in the way the molecules and atoms of our bodies take hold of hands and perform their mystic dances in the inner temple of life" (*The Breath of Life*). Maybe meditation begins and ends with this understanding. Since meditation is not a religious practice so much as a thoughtful disposition of active waiting, listening, awareness of what is present before the senses (including the sense of Reason), meditation is an apt forest in which to view the heart of John Burroughs. Here we taste the water in a stream, look on the glory of mountains, listen to the birdsongs, touch the bark of ancient wood, all while reminded of the relations, the universal context in which we live and move and have our being. What we read is not chicken soup but chili and brew for the soul.

John Burroughs draws an audience but he deserves more. He was an exemplar of inquisitive thinking and simple living—the prerequisites for honest, grounded natural spirituality. He will be fully honored when we become active participants in the simple and honest life, in our own emergence out of myopic ignorance, when we take our own evolution seriously enough to step out into the light of day, to accept the universe in some sense as he perceived that universe. We ought to honor this *reasonably simple* naturalist not because his vision was higher than ours or his scientific religion superior. On the contrary. Burroughs, like all great and lasting spiritual explorers, merely opened the doors of the old religions to point a lighter, more accessible way. Not an easier path but more illumined. To venture along his path, and discover our own, we need only leave the gods of our own making behind to smolder in the dark, to saunter free in the fresh air and limitless landscapes of this divine cosmos with Nature as our abiding companion.

Chris Highland
Whidbey Island, Washington
Autumn, 2007

Sources for the Introduction

1. *Accepting the Universe*, John Burroughs, 1920, pp. 252; 316; 121; 274.

2. *Our Friend John Burroughs*, Clara Barrus, 1914, p. 56.

3. *Field and Study*, John Burroughs, 1919, pp. 195; 197; 243; 250.

4. *The Light of Day,* John Burroughs, 1904, pp. 78; 145-146.

5. *The Breath of Life,* John Burroughs, 1915, pp. 22-23.

1

The Beginning of Things

In traversing the shores of this wild, desolate lake, I was conscious of a slight thrill of expectation, as if some secret of Nature might here be revealed, or some rare and unheard-of game disturbed. There is ever a lurking suspicion that the beginning of things is in some way associated with water, and one may notice that in his private walks he is led by a curious attraction to fetch all the springs and ponds in his route, as if by them was the place for wonders and miracles to happen.

. . .

Pressing on through the forest, after many adventures with the pine-knots, we reached, about the middle of the afternoon, our destination, Nate's Pond—a pretty sheet of water, lying like a silver mirror in the lap of the mountain, about a mile long and half a mile wide, surrounded by dark forests of balsam, hemlock, and pine, and, like the one we had just passed, a very picture of unbroken solitude.

It is not in the woods alone to give one this impression of utter loneliness. In the woods are sounds and voices, and a mute kind of companionship; one is little more than a walking tree himself; but come upon one of these mountain lakes, and the wildness stands revealed and meets you face to face. Water is thus facile and adaptive, that it makes the wild more wild, while it enhances culture and art.

Wake-Robin (1871)

***

"During these moments, a profound comfort
spreads through me,
as I look at the island, the forest, and the stream,
realizing I can never be separated from them,
can never be alone, can never fall away."
~Richard Nelson
The Island Within

2
The Gathering

One has only to sit down in the woods or the fields, or by the shore of the river or the lake and nearly everything of interest will come round to him—the birds, the animals, the insects; and presently, after his eye has got accustomed to the light and shade, he will probably see some plant or flower that he has sought in vain.... So, on a large scale, the student and lover of nature has this advantage over people who gad up and down the world, seeking some novelty or excitement; he has only to stay at home and see the procession pass. The great globe swings around to him like a revolving showcase; the change of seasons is like the passage of strange and new countries; the zones of the earth, with all their beauties and marvels, pass one's door, and linger long in the passing.

Signs and Seasons (1886)

***

"O Nature,
all that your seasons bring is fruit for me.
From thee come all things;
in thee do all things live and grow;
and to thee do all things return."
~Marcus Aurelius
Meditations

3
To Open Another Eye

Noting how one eye seconds and reinforces the other, I have often amused myself by wondering what the effect would be if one could go on opening eye after eye to the number say of a dozen or more. What would he see? Perhaps not the invisible—not the odors of flowers or the fever germs in the air—not the infinitely small of the microscope or the infinitely distant of the telescope. This would require, not more eyes so much as an eye constructed with more and different lenses; but would he not see with augmented power within the natural limits of vision? At any rate, some persons [like Thoreau] seem to have opened more eyes than others, they see with such force and distinctness; their vision penetrates the tangle and obscurity where that of others fails like a spent or impotent bullet.... Not outward eyes, but inward. We open another eye whenever we see beyond the first general features or outlines of things—whenever we grasp the special details and characteristic markings that this mask covers. Science confers new powers of vision. Whenever you have learned to discriminate the birds, or the plants, or the geological features of a country, it is as if new and keener eyes were added.

Of course one must not only see sharply, but read aright what he sees. The facts in the life of Nature that are transpiring about us are like written words that the observer is to arrange into sentences. Or the writing is in cipher and he must furnish the key.

...

The habit of observation is the habit of clear and decisive gazing: not by a first casual glance, but by a steady, deliberate aim of the eye, are the rare and characteristic things discovered. You must look intently, and hold your eye firmly to the spot, to see more than do the rank and file of humankind.... This is just as necessary to the naturalist as to the artist or the poet. The sharp eye notes specific points and differences—it seizes upon and preserves the individuality of the thing.

...

Most of the facts of nature, especially in the life of the birds and animals, are well screened. We do not see the play because we do not look intently enough.

Locusts and Wild Honey (1904)

***

"Biomimicry's ultimate goal {is}
to learn more respect for nature
and to recapture our sense of wonder.
At its best, biomimicry should take us aback,
make us more humble,
and put us in the learner's chair,
seeking to discover and emulate
instead of invent."
~Janine Benyus
Biomimicry: Innovation Inspired by Nature

4
Weather

Then the weather is that phase of Nature in which she appears not the immutable fate we are so wont to regard her, but on the contrary something quite human and changeable...a creature of moods, of caprices, of cross purposes; gloomy and downcast today, and all light and joy tomorrow; caressing and tender one moment, and severe and frigid the next; one day iron, the next day vapor; inconsistent, inconstant, incalculable; full of genius, full of folly, full of extremes; to be read and understood, not by rule, but by subtle signs and indirections—by a look, a glance, a presence, as we read and understand a man or a woman. Some days are like a rare poetic mood. There is a felicity and an exhilaration about them from morning till night. They are positive and fill one with celestial fire. Other days are negative and drain one of his electricity.

. . .

But I am not going to abuse the weather; rather to praise it, and make some amends for the many ill-natured things I have said, within hearing of the clouds, when I have been caught in the rain or been parched and withered by the drought.

Locusts and Wild Honey (1904)

***

"they have wonderful stories
of when they were young—
the important weather,
the wandering crows.
Don't be afraid to ask them questions!"
~Mary Oliver
"The Sunflowers"

5
Thinking like an Eagle

Many times during the season I have in my solitude a visit from the bald eagle. There is a dead tree near the summit, where he often perches, and which we call the "old eagle-tree." It is a pine, killed years ago by a thunderbolt—the bolt of Jove—and now the bird of Jove hovers about it or sits upon it. I have little doubt that what attracted me to this spot attracts him—the seclusion, the savageness, the elemental grandeur.

. . .

I want...to feel the inspiration of his presence and noble bearing. I want my interest and sympathy to go with him in his continental voyaging up and down, and in his long, elevated flights to and from his eyrie upon the remote solitary cliffs. He draws great lines across the sky; he sees the forests like a carpet beneath him, he sees the hills and valleys as folds and wrinkles in a many-colored tapestry; he sees the river as a silver belt connecting remote horizons. We climb mountain-peaks to get a glimpse of the spectacle that is hourly spread out beneath him.

Dignity, elevation, repose, are his. I would have my thoughts take as wide a sweep. I would be as far removed from the petty cares and turmoils of this noisy and blustering world.

Far and Near (1904)

***

"As when I was a child, I want to remain in the open, becoming something other than human under the sky."
~Kathleen Norris
Dakota

6

The Soaring Spirit

Probably the warble of the robin, or the call of the meadowlark or of the highhole, if they chanced to hear them, [mean nothing to some people]. If we have no associations with these sounds, they will mean very little to us. Their merit as musical performances is very slight. It is as signs of joy and love in nature, as heralds of spring, and as the spirit of the woods and fields made audible, that they appeal to us. The drumming of the woodpeckers and of the ruffed grouse give great pleasure to a countryman, though these sounds have not the quality of real music. It is the same with the call of the migrating geese or the voice of any wild thing: our pleasure in them is entirely apart from any considerations of music. Why does the wild flower, as we chance upon it in the woods or bogs, give us more pleasure than the more elaborate flower of the garden or lawn? Because it comes as a surprise, offers a greater contrast with its surroundings, and suggests a spirit in wild nature that seems to take thought of itself and to aspire to beautiful forms.

. . .

I have never yet seen a caged bird that I wanted—at least, not on account of its song—nor a wild flower that I wished to transfer to my garden. A caged skylark will sing its song sitting on a bit of turf in the bottom of the cage; but you want to stop your ears, it is so harsh and sibilant and penetrating. But up there against the morning sky, and above the wide expanse of fields, what delight we have in it! It is not the concord of sweet sounds: it is the soaring spirit of gladness and ecstasy raining down upon us from "heaven's gate."

Ways of Nature (1905)

***

"The haunting voices grew fainter and faded in distance,
but I sat on, stirred by a memory of something beautiful
and ancient and now lost—a forgotten freedom we must all
once have shared with other wild things,
which only they and the wilderness
can still recall to us, so that life becomes again,
for a time, the wonderful, sometimes frightening,
but fiercely joyous adventure it was intended to be."
~Martha Reben
A Sharing of Joy

7
Burst of Ecstasy

The sharp, reiterated, almost screeching song of the oven-bird [golden-crowned thrush], as it perches on a limb a few feet from the ground, like the words, "preacher, preacher, preacher," or "teacher, teacher, teacher," uttered louder and louder, and repeated six or seven times, is also familiar to most ears; but its wild, ringing, rapturous burst of song in the air high above the tree-tops is not so well known. From a very prosy, tiresome, unmelodious singer, it is suddenly transformed for a brief moment into a lyric poet of great power. It is a great surprise.... Surely it is an ordinary, commonplace bird. But wait till the inspiration of its flight-song is upon it. What a change! Up it goes through the branches of the trees, leaping from limb to limb, faster and faster, till it shoots from the tree-tops fifty or more feet into the air above them, and bursts into an ecstasy of song, rapid, ringing, lyrical; not more like its habitual performance than a match is like a rocket; brief but thrilling; emphatic but musical. Having reached its climax of flight and song, the bird closes its wings and drops nearly perpendicularly downward like the skylark. If its song were more prolonged, it would rival the song of that famous bird

.... From its habit of singing at twilight, and from the swift, darting motions of the bird, I am inclined to think that in it we have solved the mystery of Thoreau's "night-warbler," that puzzled and eluded him for years. Emerson told him he must beware of finding and booking it, lest life should have nothing more to show him.

Ways of Nature (1905)

***

"God, O Arjuna, dwells in the heart of every being
and to His delusive mystery whirls them all."
~Bhagavad Gita
The Bhagavad Gita According to Gandhi

8
Great Instinct

Ahuman being must learn to spin his web, to build his house, to sing his song, to know his food, to sail his craft, to find his way—things that the animals know "from the jump."

. . .

Instinct, I say, is a great matter, and often shames reason. It adapts means to an end, it makes few or no mistakes, it takes note of times and seasons, it delves, it bores, it spins, it weaves, it sews, it builds, it makes paper, it constructs a shelter, it navigates the air and the water, it is provident and thrifty, it knows its enemies, it outwits its foes, it crosses oceans and continents without compass, it foreshadows nearly all the arts and trades and occupations of humankind, it is skilled without practice, and wise without experience. How it arose, what its genesis was, who can tell?

. . .

What humans store in language and in books—the accumulated results of experience—the animals seem to have stored in instinct. As Darwin says, a man cannot, on his first trial, make a stone hatchet or a canoe through his power of imitation. "He has to learn his work by practice; a beaver, on the other hand, can make its dam or canal, and a bird its nest, as well or nearly as well, and a spider its wonderful web quite as well, the first time it tries as when old and experienced."

Ways of Nature (1905)

***

"There is nothing—not even the tiniest thing—
that is not fastened
to the links of this chain."
~Moses de Leon
The Chain of Being

9
Fear

Fear, like joy or curiosity, is contagious among beasts and birds, as it is among people; the young fox or wolf would instantly share the emotion of its parent in the presence of a trap. It is very important to the wild creatures that they have a quick apprehension of danger, and as a matter of fact they have. One wild and suspicious duck in a flock will often defeat the best laid plans of the duck-hunter. Its suspicions are quickly communicated to all its fellows: not through any conscious effort on its part to do so, but through the law of natural contagion.... Where any bird or beast is much hunted, fear seems to be in the air, and their fellows come to be conscious of the danger which they have not experienced.

What an animal lacks in wit it makes up in caution. Fear is a good thing for the wild creatures to have in superabundance. It often saves them from real danger. But how undiscriminating it is!

. . .

Animals are afraid on general principles. Anything new and strange excites their suspicions. In a herd of animals, cattle, or horses, fear quickly becomes a panic and rages like a conflagration. Cattlemen in the West found that any little thing at night might kindle the spark in their herds and sweep the whole mass away in a furious stampede. Each animal excites every other, and the multiplied fear of the herd is something terrible. Panics among people are not much different.

Ways of Nature (1905)

***

*"I steer my bark with Hope in the {bow},
leaving Fear astern."*
~Thomas Jefferson
Letter to John Adams, April 8, 1816

10
Over the Pasture Wall

One of my critics has accused me of measuring all things by the standard of my little farm—of thinking that what is not true of animal life there is not true anywhere. Unfortunately my farm *is* small—hardly twenty acres—and its animal life very limited. I have never seen even a porcupine upon it; but I have a hill where one might roll down, should one ever come my way and be in the mood for that kind of play. I have a few possums, a woodchuck or two, an occasional skunk, some red squirrels and rabbits, and many kinds of songbirds. Foxes occasionally cross my acres; and once, at least, I saw a bald eagle devouring a fish in one of my apple-trees. Wild ducks, geese, and swans in spring and fall pass across the sky above me. Quail and grouse invade my premises, and of crows I have, at least in bird-nesting time, too many.

But I have a few times climbed over my pasture wall and wandered into distant fields. Once upon a time I was a traveler in Asia for the space of two hours—an experience that ought to have yielded me some startling discoveries, but did not. Indeed, the wider I have traveled and observed nature, the more I am convinced that the wild creatures behave just about the same in all parts of the country; that is, under similar conditions.

What one observes truly about bird or beast upon his farm of ten acres, he will not have to unlearn, travel as wide or as far as he will.

Ways of Nature (1905)

***

"I felt that if I stayed much longer in {my hometown},
I would be covered with hair and moss.
I roamed the streets, I searched and prayed:
'God, Thou who hidest in the clouds
or behind the shoemaker's house,
grant that my soul may be revealed,
the sorrowful soul of a stammering boy.
Show me my way. I do not want to be like all the others;
I want to see a new world.'"
~Marc Chagall
My Life

11
Beauty in a Mountain Stream

My eyes had never before beheld such beauty in a mountain stream. The water was almost as transparent as the air,-was, indeed, like liquid air; and as it lay in these wells and pits enveloped in shadow, or lit up by a chance ray of the vertical sun, it was a perpetual feast to the eye, -so cool, so deep, so pure; every reach and pool like a vast spring. You lay down and drank or dipped the water up in your cup, and found it just the right degree of refreshing coldness. One is never prepared for the clearness of the water in these streams. It is always a surprise. See them every year for a dozen years, and yet, when you first come upon one, you will utter an exclamation. I saw nothing like it in the Adirondacks, nor in Canada. Absolutely without stain or hint of impurity, it seems to magnify like a lens, so that the bed of the stream and the fish in it appear deceptively near. It is rare to find even a trout stream that is not a little "off color," as they say of diamonds, but the waters in the section of which I am writing have the genuine ray; it is the undimmed and untarnished diamond.

In the Catskills (1910)

***

"So must I stay for a long time
Until I have grown from the rock
And the stream is running through me
And I cannot tell myself from one tall tree.
...
My help is in the mountain
That I take away with me."
~Nancy Wood
"My Help is in the Mountain"
Hollering Sun

12
An Exhilarating Walk

How elastic and exhilarating the walk was through the cool, transparent shadows! The sun was gilding the mountains, and its yellow light seemed to be reflected through all the woods. At one point we looked through and along a valley of deep shadow upon a broad sweep of mountain quite near and densely clothed with woods, flooded from base to summit by the setting sun. It was a wild, memorable scene. What power and effectiveness in Nature, I thought, and how rarely an artist catches her touch! Looking down upon or squarely into a mountain covered with a heavy growth of birch and maple, and shone upon by the sun, is a sight peculiarly agreeable to me. How closely the swelling umbrageous heads of the trees fit together, and how the eye revels in the flowing and easy uniformity, while the mind feels the ruggedness and terrible power beneath!

In the Catskills (1910)

***

*"Closer observation will reveal to us
the beauty and excellence of simplicity,
a quality as yet too little valued or understood in this country.
And when we have made this farther progress,
then we shall take better care of our trees."*
~Susan Fennimore Cooper
Rural Hours

13
These Mountains We Behold

These mountains we behold and cross are not picturesque, -they are wild and inhuman as the sea. In them you are in a maze, in a weltering world of woods; you can see neither the earth nor the sky, but a confusion of the growth and decay of centuries, and must traverse them by your compass or your science of woodcraft, -a rift through the trees giving one a glimpse of the opposite range or of the valley beneath, and he is more at sea than ever; one does not know his own farm or settlement when framed in these mountain treetops; all look alike unfamiliar.

. . .

The Arabs believe that the mountains steady the earth and hold it together; but they have only to get on the top of a high one to see how insignificant mountains are, and how adequate the earth looks to get along without them. To the imaginative Oriental people, mountains seemed to mean much more than they do to us. They were sacred; they were the abodes of their divinities. They offered their sacrifices upon them. In the Bible, mountains are used as a symbol of that which is great and holy. Jerusalem is spoken of as a holy mountain. The Syrians were beaten by the Children of Israel because, said they, "their gods are gods of the hills; therefore were they stronger than we." It was on Mount Horeb that God appeared to Moses in the burning bush, and on Sinai that He delivered to him the law. Josephus says that the Hebrew shepherds never pasture their flocks on Sinai, believing it to be the abode of Jehovah. The solitude of mountain-tops is peculiarly impressive, and it is certainly easier to believe the Deity appeared in a burning bush there than in the valley below. When the clouds of heaven, too, come down and envelop the top of the mountain, -how such a circumstance must have impressed the old God-fearing Hebrews! Moses knew well how to surround the law with the pomp and circumstance that would inspire the deepest awe and reverence.

In the Catskills (1910)

***

> *"Good people shine from afar,*
> *like the Snowy Mountains."*
> ~Gautama Buddha
> *Dhammapada*

14
Hemlocks

The ancient hemlocks, whither I propose to take the reader, are rich in many things besides birds. Indeed, their wealth in this respect is owing mainly, no doubt, to their rank vegetable growths, their fruitful swamps, and their dark, sheltered retreats.

Their history is of an heroic cast. Ravished and torn by the tanner in his thirst for bark, preyed upon by the lumberman, assaulted and beaten back by the settler, still their spirit has never been broken, their energies never paralyzed. Not many years ago a public highway passed through them, but it was at no time a tolerable road; trees fell across it, mud and limbs choked it up, till finally travelers took the hint and went around; and now, walking along its deserted course, I see only the footprints of coons, foxes, and squirrels.

Nature loves such woods, and places her own seal upon them. Here she shows me what can be done with ferns and mosses and lichens. The soil is marrowy and full of innumerable forests. Standing in these fragrant aisles, I feel the strength of the vegetable kingdom, and am awed by the deep and inscrutable processes of life going on so silently about me.

. . .

Mounting toward the upland again, I pause reverently as the hush and stillness of twilight come upon the woods. It is the sweetest, ripest hour of the day. And as the hermit's evening

hymn goes up from the deep solitude below me, I experience that serene exaltation of sentiment of which music, literature, and religion are but the faint types and symbols. (1865)
In the Catskills (1910)

***

"What's rare in that real world, and common here,
is the chance for completion.
For being big sometimes and small at others,
in the shadow of the mountains
and the shade of the hemlocks."
~Bill McKibben
Wandering Home

15
What is a Bird without its Song?

June, of all the months, the student of ornithology can least afford to lose. Most birds are nesting then, and in full song and plumage. And what is a bird without its song? Do we not wait for the stranger to speak? It seems to me that I do not know a bird till I have heard its voice; then I come nearer it at once, and it possesses a human interest to me. I have met the gray-cheeked thrush in the woods, and held him in my hand; still I do not know him. The silence of the cedar-bird throws a mystery about him which neither his good looks nor his petty larcenies in cherry time can dispel. A bird's song contains a clew to its life, and establishes a sympathy, an understanding, between itself and the listener.

. . .

I descend a steep hill, and approach the hemlocks through a large sugar-bush. When twenty rods distant, I hear all along the line of the forest the incessant warble of the red-eyed vireo, cheerful and happy as the merry whistle of a schoolboy. He is one of our most common and widely distributed birds. Approach any forest at any hour of the day, in any kind of weather, from May to August, in any of the Middle or Eastern districts, and the chances are that the first note you hear will be his. Rain or shine, before noon or after, in the deep forest or in the village grove,-when it is too hot for the thrushes or too cold and windy for the warblers, -it is never out of time or place for this little minstrel to indulge his cheerful strain. In the deep wilds of the Adirondacks, where few birds are seen and fewer heard, his note was almost constantly in my ear. Always busy, making it a point never to suspend for one moment his occupation to indulge his musical taste, his lay is that of industry and contentment. There is nothing plaintive or especially musical in his performance, but the sentiment expressed is eminently that of cheerfulness. Indeed, the songs of most birds have some human significance, which, I think, is the source of the delight we take in them. The song of the bobolink to me expresses hilarity; the song sparrow's, faith; the bluebird's, love; the catbird's, pride; the white-eyed flycatcher's, self-consciousness; that of the hermit thrush, spiritual serenity: while there is something military in the call of the robin.

In the Catskills (1910)

***

"*Sing on, sweet thrush, upon the leafless bough,*
Sing on, sweet bird, I listen to thy strain,
See aged Winter, 'mid his surly reign
At thy blythe carol, clears his furrowed brow."
~Robert Burns
"*On Hearing a Thrush Sing in a Morning Walk*"
(*January 25, 1793*)

16
Wild Tracks

I walk along the old road, and note the tracks in the thin layer of mud. When do these creatures travel here? I have never yet chanced to meet one. Here a partridge has set its foot; there, a woodcock; here, a squirrel or mink; there, a skunk; there, a fox. What a clear, nervous track reynard makes! how easy to distinguish it from that of a little dog,-it is so sharply cut and defined! A dog's track is coarse and clumsy beside it. There is as much wildness in the track of an animal as in its voice. Is a deer's track like a sheep's or a goat's? What winged-footed fleetness and agility may be inferred from the sharp, braided track of the gray squirrel upon the new snow! Ah! in nature is the best discipline. How wood-life sharpens the senses, giving a new power to the eye, the ear, the nose! And are not the rarest and most exquisite songsters wood-birds?

In the Catskills (1910)

***

"If you have no relationship with nature
you have no relationship with humanity.
Nature is the meadows, the groves, the rivers,
all the marvelous earth, the trees, and the beauty of the earth.
If we have no relationship with that,
we shall have no relationship with each other."
~J. Krishnamurti
All the Marvelous Earth

17

The Angling Heart

I have been a seeker of trout from my boyhood, and on all the expeditions in which this fish has been the ostensible purpose I have brought home more game than my creel showed. In fact, in my mature years I find I got more of nature into me, more of the woods, the wild, nearer to bird and beast, while threading my native streams for trout, than in almost any other way. It furnished a good excuse to go forth; it pitched one in the right key; it sent one through the fat and marrowy places of field and wood. Then the fisherman has a harmless, preoccupied look; he is a kind of vagrant that nothing fears. He blends himself with the trees and the shadows. All his approaches are gentle and indirect. He times himself to the meandering, soliloquizing stream; its impulse bears him along. At the foot of the waterfall he sits sequestered and hidden in its volume of sound. The birds know he has no designs upon them, and the animals see that his mind is in the creek. His enthusiasm anneals him, and makes him pliable to the scenes and influences he moves among.

Then what acquaintance he makes with the stream! He addresses himself to it as a lover to his mistress; he wooes it and stays with it till he knows its most hidden secrets. It runs through his thoughts not less than through its banks there; he feels the fret and thrust of every bar and boulder. Where it deepens, his purpose deepens; where it is shallow, he is indifferent. He knows how to interpret its every glance and dimple; its beauty haunts him for days.

...

But I early learned that from almost any stream in a trout country the true angler could take trout, and that the great secret was this, that, whatever bait you used, worm, grasshopper, grub, or fly, there was one thing you must always put upon your hook, namely, your heart.

In the Catskills (1910)

***

*"There is value in any experience that reminds us
of our dependency on the soil-plant-animal-{human}
food chain, and of the fundamental organization
of the biota."*
~Aldo Leopold
A Sand County Almanac

18
The Key to the Secret

I crave and seek a natural explanation of all phenomena upon this earth, but the word "natural" to me implies more than mere chemistry and physics. The birth of a baby, and the blooming of a flower, are natural events, but the laboratory methods forever fail to give us the key to the secret of either.

I am forced to conclude that my passion for nature and for all open-air life, though tinged and stimulated by science, is not a passion for pure science, but for literature and philosophy. My imagination and ingrained humanism are appealed to by the facts and methods of natural history. I find something akin to poetry and religion...in the shows of day and night, and in my excursions to fields and woods. The love of nature is a different thing from the love of science, though the two may go together.... To the rigid man of science this is frank mysticism; but without a sense of the unknown and unknowable, life is flat and barren. Without the emotion of the beautiful, the sublime, the mysterious, there is no art, no religion, no literature.

. . .

We are all made of one stuff undoubtedly, vegetable and animal, man and woman, dog and donkey, and the secret of the difference between us, and of the passing along of the difference from generation to generation with but slight variations, may be…in the way the molecules and atoms of our bodies take hold of hands and perform their mystic dances in the inner temple of life.

The Breath of Life (1915)

***

"I celebrate myself, and sing myself,
And what I assume you shall assume,
For every atom belonging to me
as good belongs to you…
every atom of my blood,
form'd from this soil, this air."
~Walt Whitman
"Song of Myself"

19
Scent of an Atom

No human eye has ever seen, or will see, an atom; only the mind's eye, or the imagination, sees atoms and molecules....

Only two of our senses make us acquainted with matter in a state which may be said to approach the atomic—smell and taste. Odors are material emanations, and represent a division of matter into inconceivably small particles. What are the perfumes we smell but emanations, flying atoms or electrons, radiating in all directions, and continuing for a shorter or longer time without any appreciable diminution in bulk or weight of the substances that give them off? How many millions or trillions of times does the rose divide its heart in the perfume it sheds so freely upon the air? The odor of the musk of certain animals lingers under certain conditions for years. The imagination is baffled in trying to conceive of the number and minuteness of the particles which the fox leaves of itself in the snow where its foot was imprinted—so palpable that the scent of a hound can seize upon them hours after the fox has passed! The all but infinite divisibility of matter is proved by every odor that the breeze brings us from field and wood, and by the delicate flavors that the tongue detects in the food we eat and drink....

When we smell an apple or a flower, we probably get a real fragment of the apple, or of the flower....

The Breath of Life (1915)

***

"You are the forest; you are all the great trees in the forest;
you are the bird and beast playing in and out of all the trees;
O lord white as jasmine, filling and filled by all
why don't you show me your face?"
~Akkamahadevi
"The Lord White as Jasmine"

20
Nature's Machines

The mechanical conception of life repels us because of its association in our minds with the fabrications of our own hands—the dead metal and wood and the noise and dust of our machine-ridden and machine-produced civilization.

But Nature makes no machines like our own. She uses mechanical principles everywhere, in inert matter and in living bodies, but she does not use them in the bald and literal way we do. We must divest her mechanisms of the rigidity and angularity that pertain to the works of our own hands. Her hooks and hinges and springs and sails and coils and airplanes, all involve mechanical contrivances, but how differently they impress us from our own application of the same principles! Even in inert matter—in the dews, the rains, the winds, the tides, the snows, the streams—her mechanics and her chemistry and her hydrostatics and pneumatics, seem much nearer akin to life than our own. We must remember that Nature's machines are not human machines. When we place our machine so that it is driven by the great universal currents—the wheel in the stream, the sail on the water—the result is much more pleasing and poetic than when propelled by artificial power.

The more machinery we get between ourselves and Nature, the farther off Nature seems.... No machine we have ever made or seen can wind itself up, or has life....

The Breath of Life (1915)

***

"We thought it made perfectly good sense
to transport salmon in trucks on the highway,
so that grain and petroleum could move in barges on the river.
We thought we needed power and wealth,
but we discovered to our sorrow that what we really need
are health and beauty and a way of life that
listens to the land."
~Kathleen Dean Moore
"Amazing Grace"
in *Audubon magazine, March/April 2001*

21
The Divinity of Matter

Our reason demands that the natural order be all-inclusive. Can our faith in the divinity of matter measure up to this standard? Not till we free ourselves from the inherited prejudices which have grown up from our everyday struggles with [material things]. We must follow the guidance of science till we penetrate this husk and see its real mystical and transcendental character.

No deductions of science can satisfy our longings for something kindred to our own spirits in the universe. But neither our telescopes nor our microscopes reveal such a reality. Is this longing only the result of our inevitable anthropomorphism, or is it the evidence of things unseen, the substance of things hoped for, the prophecy of our kinship with the farthest star? Can soul arise out of a soulless universe?

Though the secret of life is under our feet, yet how strange and mysterious it seems! It draws our attention away from matter.... We are so immersed in these realities [of matter, energy and consciousness] that we do not see the divinity they embody. We call that sacred and divine which is far off and unattainable. Life and mind are so impossible [to be explained] in terms of matter and energy, that it is [no wonder] that humans have so long looked upon their appearance upon this earth as a miraculous event. But until science opened our eyes we did not know that the celestial and the terrestrial are one, and that we are already in the heavens among the stars. When we emancipate ourselves...and see with clear vision our relations to the Cosmos, all our ideas of materialism and spiritualism are made over, and we see how the two are one; how life and death play into each other's hands, and how the whole truth of things cannot be compassed by any number of finite minds.

The Breath of Life (1915)

***

"Who are you, Nature?
I live in you;
for fifty years I have been seeking you,
and I have not found you yet."
~Voltaire
Philosophical Dictionary

22

Mysteries Enough for a Lifetime

One sees with the mind's eye this stream of energy, which we name the material universe.... Life is inseparable from this river of energy.

In midsummer what river-men call "the blossoming of the water" takes place in the Hudson River; the water is full of minute vegetable organisms; they are seasonal and temporary; they are born of the midsummer heats. By and by the water is clear again. Life in the universe seems as seasonal and fugitive as this blossoming of the water.... One need not go away from his own doorstep to find mysteries enough to last him a lifetime, but he will find them in his own body, in the ground upon which he stands, not less than in his mind, and in the invisible forces that play around him. We may marvel how the delicate color and perfume of the flower could come by way of the root and stalk of the plant, or how the crude mussel could give birth to the rainbow-tinted pearl...or how the ugly worm wakes up and finds itself a winged creature of the air; yet we do not invoke the supernatural to account for these things....

The spiritual always has its root and genesis in the physical. We do not degrade the spiritual in such a conception; we open our eyes to the spirituality of the physical. And this is what science has always been doing and is doing more and more—making us familiar with marvelous and transcendent powers that hedge us about and enter into every act of our lives. The more we know matter, the more we know mind; the more we know nature, the more we know God; the more familiar we are with the earth forces, the more intimate will be our acquaintance with the celestial forces.

The Breath of Life (1915)

***

"We can never be so certain...of any miracle,
or the design of any miracle,
as we are from the revelation of nature,
i.e., Nature's God."
~John Adams
Letter to Thomas Jefferson, September 14, 1813

23
Currents of the Globe

The migrating wild creatures, whether birds or beasts, always arrest the attention. They seem to link up animal life with the great currents of the globe. It is moving day on a continental scale. It is the call of the primal instinct to increase and multiply, suddenly setting in motion whole tribes and races....

. . .

That birds have a sense of home and return in most cases to their old haunts, is quite certain....

. . .

One sees the passing bird procession in his own grounds and neighborhood without pausing to think that in every man's grounds and in every neighborhood throughout the States, and throughout a long, broad belt of States, about several millions of homes, and over several millions of farms, the same flood-tide of bird-life is creeping and eddying or sweeping over the land.

. . .

The waves of bird migrants roll on through the States into Canada and beyond, breaking like waves on the shore, and spreading their contents over large areas....

...

Nature is a sort of outlying province of ourselves. We feel a kinship with her works, and in bird and beast, in tree and flower, we behold the workings of the same life principle that has brought us where we are and relates us to all living things.

Field and Study (1919)

***

"To the heart of Nature one must...be drawn in such a life;
and very soon I learned how richly she repays
in deep refreshment the reverent love of her worshipper."
~Celia Laighton Thaxter
Among the Isles of Shoals

24
Teach the Children

Once started in pursuit of nature lore, we are pretty sure to keep on. When people ask me, "How shall we teach our children to love nature?" I reply: "Do not try to teach them at all. Just turn them loose in the country and trust to luck." It is time enough to answer children's questions when they are interested enough to ask them. Knowledge without love does not stick; but if love comes first, knowledge is pretty sure to follow. I do not know how I first got my own love for nature, but I suppose it was because I was born and passed my youth on the farm, and reacted spontaneously to the natural objects about me. I felt a certain privacy and kinship with the woods and fields and streams long before the naturalist awoke to self-consciousness within me. A feeling of companionship with Nature came long prior to any conscious desire for accurate and specific knowledge about her works. I loved the flowers and the wild creatures, as most healthy children do, long before I knew there was such a study as botany or natural history. And when I take a walk now, thoughts of natural history play only a secondary part; I suspect it is more to bathe the spirit in natural influences than to store the mind with natural facts.

I think I know what Emerson means when he says elsewhere in his Journal that a walk in the woods is one of the secrets for dodging old age.

Field and Study (1919)

***

"Nature never became a toy to a wise spirit.
The flowers, the animals, the mountains,
reflected the wisdom of his best hour,
as much as they had delighted
the simplicity of his childhood."
~Ralph Waldo Emerson
Nature

25

On Intimate Terms

Many a walk I take in the fields and woods when I gather no new facts and make no new observations; and yet I feel enriched. I have been for an hour or more on intimate terms with trees and rocks and grass and birds and with "Nature's primal sanities;" the fragrance of the wild things lingers about my mind for days.

Yet the close observation of nature, the training of the eye and mind to read her signals, to penetrate her screens, to disentangle her skeins, to catch her significant facts, add greatly to the pleasure of a walk and to life in the country. Natural history is on the wing, and all about us on the foot. It hides in holes, it perches on trees, it runs to cover under the stones and into the stone walls; it soars, it sings, it drums, it calls by day, it barks and prowls and hoots by night. It eats your fruit, it plunders your garden, it raids your henroost, and maybe disturbs your midnight slumbers.

. . .

All such things add interest to country life. No wild creature comes amiss, even though it rob your henroost. I sometimes grow tender toward the woodchuck, even though he raids my garden; he is such a characteristic bit of wild nature, creeping about the fields, or sitting upon his haunches to see if danger is near. He is of the earth, earthy, its true offspring, steeped in its savors, hugging it close, harmonizing with its soil and rocks, almost as liquid as its fountains and as perennial as its grass.

Field and Study (1919)

***

"While he was thinking one thing in his brain,
I was endeavoring to divine his thought in mine.
It was a pretty game, played on
the smooth surface of the pond,
a man against a loon."
~Henry David Thoreau
"Brute Neighbors"
Walden

26
Seeds at the Door

The winged seeds always find their proper habitat, as if they had eyes to see the way. The seeds of the cat-tail flag find the ditches and marshes as unerringly as if they were convoyed. But this intelligence, or self-direction, is only apparent. The wind carries the seeds in all directions, and they fall everywhere, just as it happens, on the hills as well as in the ditches, but only in the latter do they take root and flourish. Nature often resorts to this wholesale method. In scattering pollen and germs by the aid of the wind, this is her method: cover all the ground, and you will be sure to hit your mark night or day.

After one or more windy days in November I am sure to find huddled in the recess of my kitchen door the branching heads of a certain species of wild grass that grows somewhere on the hills west of me. These heads find their ways across fields and highways, over fences, past tree and bushy barriers, down my steps, into the storm-house, and lie there, waiting on the doorsill like things of life, waiting to get into the house. Not one season alone, but every season, they come as punctually as the assessor. The watchful broom routs them; but the next day or the next week there they are again, and now and then one actually gets into the kitchen, slipping in between your feet as you open the door. They bring word from over the hills, and the word is: "Sooner or later Nature hits her mark, hits all marks, because her aim is broadcast and her efforts ceaseless. The wind finds every crack and corner. We started on our journey not for your door, but for any door, all doors, any shelter where we could be at rest; and here we are!"

Field and Study (1919)

***

"Wind she brews a heady kettle.
Human beings love it—love it.
Gods above are not above it."
~Robert Frost
"Clear and Colder"

27
Lightning

We see the lightning cleave the air in one blinding flash from the clouds to the earth, often shattering a tree or a house on its way down. Hence it is always a surprise to see the evidence that the thunderbolt strikes upward as well as downward. During an electric storm one summer night an enormous charge of electricity came up out of the earth under a maple-tree at the foot of the hill below my study, scattering the sod, the roots, and some small bushes like an explosion of powder or dynamite; then it rooted around on the ground like a pig, devouring or annihilating the turf, making a wide, ragged, zigzag trench seven or eight feet long down the hill in the ground, when it dived beneath the wagon track, five or six feet wide, bursting out here and there on the surface, then escaped out of the bank made by the plough on the edge of the vineyard. Here it seems to have leaped to the wire trellis of the grapevines, running along it northward, scorching the leaves here and there, and finally vented its fury on a bird-box that was fastened to a post at the end of the row. It completely demolished the box, going a foot or more out of its way to do so. The box was not occupied, so there was not the anticlimax of a bolt of Jove slaughtering house wrens or bluebirds. Maybe it was the nails that drew the charge to the box. But why it was rooting around down the hill when it came out of the ground, instead of leaping upward, is a puzzle.

It acted like some blind, crazy material body that did not know where to go. A cannon-shot would have made a much smoother trench. Its course on the ground was about twelve or fourteen feet, half above and half below ground, and its leap in the air about six feet. Strange that a thing of such incredible speed and power should yet have time to loiter about and do such "fool stunts"! [The bolt] left a trail like a slow, plodding thing. It burrowed like a mole, it delved like a plough, it leaped and ran like a squirrel, and it struck like a hammer. A spectator would have been aware only of a blinding blaze of fire there on the edge of the vineyard, and heard a crash that would have stunned him; but probably could not have told whether the bolt came upward or downward. Lightning is much quicker than our special senses.

Field and Study (1919)

***

"There shines not the sun, neither moon nor star,
Nor flash of lightning, nor fire lit on earth.
The Self is the light reflected by all."
~Katha Upanishad

28
Nest of Gold

In walking along a secluded, bushy lane leading to the woods, which has been a favorite walk of mine for more than forty years, I chanced upon another secret treasure open to the eye of heaven, which gave me a degree of pleasure greater than any other single incident which my forty years' acquaintance with the old lane had brought me. Encircled by the stalks of a tall-growing weed, I chanced to see upon the ground a deep, bulky, beautifully formed nest. It was a mass of dry leaves and grasses, with an unusually deep and smooth cavity lined with very fine vegetable fibre that looked like gold thread. Evidently a finished nest, I thought, but it was empty, and there were no birds about. It did not have the appearance of a nest that had been "harried," as the Scotch boys say, but of one just that moment finished and waiting for its first egg. A week later I returned to the place and was delighted to find that it was really a live nest. The setting bird had slipped off on my approach so slyly that I had not seen her. The nest contained four small, delicate white eggs marked with fine black specks on their larger ends; these were completely dominated by a large, vulgar-looking cowbird's egg. Presently two anxious birds, one of them strikingly marked with yellow, black, white, and blue-gray, appeared in the branches above my head, and began peering nervously down upon me and uttering a faint "sip," "sip." "Warblers," I said; and, as they flitted excitedly about me,

I soon recognized the golden-winged warbler—a rare bird in my locality, and one whose nest I had never before seen. "What a pretty coincidence," I said—"the nest of the golden-winged warbler at the foot of a clump of goldenrod, and lined with gold thread!" The old, neglected farm lane had never before yielded me such a treasure.

Field and Study (1919)

***

"Do they not observe the birds above them,
Spreading their wings and folding them in?
None can uphold them except The Most Gracious:
Truly it is He that watches over all things."
~Qur'an

29
A Feathered Edge

Probably we have no other familiar bird keyed up to the same degree of intensity as the house wren. He seems to be the one bird whose cup of life is always overflowing. The wren is habitually in an ecstasy either of delight or of rage. He probably gets on the nerves of more persons than any other of our birds. He is so shrilly and overflowingly joyous, or else so sharply and harshly angry and pugnacious—a lyrical burst one minute, and a volley of chiding, staccato notes the next. More restless than the wind, he is a tiny dynamo of bird energy. From his appearance in May till his last brood is out in midsummer, he repeats his shrill, hurried little strain about ten times a minute for about ten hours a day, and cackles and chatters between-times. He expends enough energy in giving expression to his happiness, or vent to his anger, in the course of each day to carry him halfway to the Gulf. He sputters, he chatters, he carols; he excites the wrath of bluebirds, phoebes, orioles, robins; he darts into holes; he bobs up in unexpected places; he nests in old hats, in dinner-pails, in pumps, in old shoes. Give him a twig and a feather and a hole in almost anything, and his cup is full. How absurdly happy he is over a few dry twigs there in that box, and his little freckled mate sitting upon her eggs! His throat swells and throbs as if he had all the winds of Aeolus imprisoned in it, and the little tempest of joy in there rages all the time. His song goes off as suddenly as if some one had touched a spring or switched on a current. If feathers can have a feathered edge, the wren has it.

Field and Study (1919)

***

"One feather is a bird,
I claim; one tree, a wood;
In her low voice I heard
More than a mortal should...

...

"Desire exults the ear:
Bird, girl, and ghostly tree,
The earth, the solid air—
Their slow song sang in me."
~Theodore Roethke
"The Voice"

30
Eve of a Great Change

As I was walking on the porch one morning in early October I chanced to see a black-and-green caterpillar about two inches long posed in a meditative attitude upon the side of the house a foot or more above the floor. The latter half of its body was attached to the board wall, and the fore part curved up from it with bowed head. The creature was motionless, and apparently absorbed in deep meditation. I stooped down and examined it more closely. I saw that it was on the eve of a great change. The surface of the board immediately under the forward part of the body had been silvered over with a very fine silken web that was almost like a wash, rather than something woven. Anchored to this on both sides, as if grown out of the web, ran a very fine thread or cord up over the caterpillar's back, which served to hold it in place; it could lean against the thread as a sailor leans against a rope thrown around him and tied to the mast. With bowed head the future butterfly hung there, and with bowed head I waited and watched.

Field and Study (1919)

***

"We use the word 'wilderness,'
but perhaps we mean wildness.
Isn't that why I've come here,
to seek the wildness in myself
and, in so doing, come on the wildness everywhere,
because after all, I'm part of nature too."
~Gretel Ehrlich
Islands, the Universe, Home

31
The Crow

When I stop to contemplate the ways of the wild creatures around me and the part they play in the all-the-year-round drama, my thoughts are pretty sure to rest for a while on the crow. From the wide distribution of the crow over the earth in some form, it would appear that Nature has him very much at heart. She has equipped him to make his way in widely diversified lands and climates. He thrives upon the shore and he thrives upon the mountains. He is not strictly a bird of prey, neither is he preyed upon. What is it in nature that he expresses? True, he expresses cunning, hardiness, sociability; but he is not alone in these things. Yet the crow is unique; he is a character, and at times one is almost persuaded that he has a vein of humor in him. Probably no country [child] who has had a tame crow has any doubt about it. His mischief-making propensities are certainly evident. His soliloquies, his deliberate cat-calls and guttural sounds, his petty tealing, his teasing of other animals, his impudent curiosity, all stamp him as a bird full of the original Adam....

His is the one voice you are pretty sure to hear wherever your walk leads you. He is at home and about his own business. It is not his grace as a flyer that pleases us; he is heavy and commonplace on the wing—no airiness, no easy mastery as with the hawks; only when he walks is he graceful. How much at home he looks upon the ground—an ebony clod-hopper, but in his bearing the lord of the soil. He always looks prosperous; he always looks contented; his voice is always reassuring. The farmer may be disgruntled and discouraged, his crows are not. The country is good enough for them; they can meet their engagements; they do not borrow trouble; they have not lived on the credit of the future; their acres are not mortgaged....

He is a bit of the night with the sheen of the stars in it, yet the open day is his province, publicity his passion. He is a spy, a policeman, a thief, a good fellow, a loyal friend, an alarmist, a socialist, all in one.... Come rain, come shine, come heat, come snow, he is on his job and is always reassuring.

Field and Study (1919)

***

"Then he looked into the air, questioning,
for overhead he heard the sharp call of a bird....
'These are my animals,' he said....
May my animals lead me!' "
~Friedrich Nietzsche
Thus Spoke Zarathustra

32
Open Book

The book of nature is always open winter and summer and is always within reach, and the print is legible if we have eyes to read it. But most persons are too preoccupied to have their attention arrested by it. Think of the amazing number of natural things and incidents that must come under the observations of the farmer, the miner, the hunter, that do not interest him, because they are aside from his main purpose. I see a farmer getting his cows every morning in the early dawn while the dew is on the grass and all nature is just waking up, and think, during the twenty or more years that he has been doing this, what interesting and significant incidents he might have witnessed in the lives of the wild creatures, if his mind had been alert to such happenings! But it was not. He noticed only his cows, or where his fences needed mending, or where a spring needed clearing out. What a harvest Thoreau would have gathered during [those years]! From ant to bumble-bee, and from bumble-bee to hawks and eagles, he would have caught the significant things....

Our interest in nature is a reflection of our interest in ourselves; nature is ourselves extended and seen externally....

. . .

Wait long enough and Nature will always have a fresh surprise for you.

...

One need never to expect to exhaust the natural history of even his own farm. Every year sees a new and enlarged edition of the book of nature, and we may never hope to turn the final leaf.

Field and Study (1919)

***

"Miles and miles of tree scripture along the sky,
a bible that will one day be read!
its letters and sentences has burned me like fire...."
~John Muir
Letter to Jeanne C. Carr, September, 1874

33
Wisdom of Insects

We have no name for [the reasoning] of insects but instinct—untaught wisdom—but in some cases it is so far beyond anything that [humans] attain to, except after long research and experimentation, that we marvel at it as we would at the supernatural. The knowledge that the hunting wasps possess that the spiders and crickets and beetles which they bring and store up for their young...must be paralyzed but not killed...how far it transcends anything we know until we call to our aid all the resources of experimental science!

. . .

O strange and baffling Nature! Truly thy ways are not as our ways. But Nature keeps the game of life going, which seems her main purpose, making it as various and picturesque as possible.

. . .

The intelligence of the insect is the intelligence of Nature—it is action and not reflection. Nature lives and grows, and does not pause to cogitate and ask the reason why, as we do. Her works are a perpetual revelation.

Field and Study (1919)

***

"{By the pond I saw a} dragonfly bouquet.
Be still, and the world is bound
to turn herself inside out to entertain you.
Everywhere you look, joyful noise is clanging
to drown out quiet desperation.
The choice is draw the blinds and shut it all out,
or believe."
~Barbara Kingsolver
High Tide in Tucson

34
The Search

The wild life around one becomes interesting the moment one gets into the current of it and sees its characteristics and by-play. The coons that come down off the mountain into my orchard for apples on the chill November nights; the fox that prowls about near me and wakens me by his wild, vulpine squall at two o'clock in the morning; the woodchucks burrowing in my meadows and eating and tangling my clover, and showing sudden terror when they spy me peeping over the stone wall or coming with my rifle; the chipmunk leaving a mound of freshly dug earth conspicuous by the roadside, while his entrance to his den is deftly concealed under the grass or strawberry-vines a few yards away; the red squirrel spinning along the stone wall, his movements apparently controlled by the electric-like waves of energy that run along his tail and impart to it a new curve or kink every moment, or chipping up my apples and pears for the seed…how much there is in the lives of all these creatures that we should find keenly interesting if we knew how to get at it!

. . .

The search for the elements of the interesting in nature and in life, in persons and in things—well, is an interesting search.

Field and Study (1919)

***

"The pervasive beauty of nature
appeals to our better instincts and inspires
reverence, awe and respect.
It lifts us out of our narrow selves
and stretches our horizons of appreciation and concern.
It reminds us of the privilege of being alive
and of being consciously aware of ourselves
and the marvelous world in which we live."
~Donald A. Crosby
A Religion of Nature

35
Where Nature Makes a Home

After long experience I am convinced that the best place to study nature is at one's own home—on the farm, in the mountains, on the plains, by the sea—no matter where that may be. One has it all about him then. The seasons bring to his door the great revolving cycle of wild life, floral and faunal, and he need miss no part of the show.

At home one should see and hear with more fondness and sympathy. Nature should touch him a little more closely there than anywhere else. He is better attuned to it than to strange scenes. The birds about his own door are his birds, the flowers in his own fields and wood are his, the rainbow springs its magic arch across his valley, even the everlasting stars to which one lifts his eye, night after night, and year after year, from his own doorstep, have something private and personal about them. The clouds and the sunsets one sees in strange lands move one the more they are like the clouds and sunsets one has become familiar with at home. The wild creatures about you become known to you as they cannot be known to a passer-by. The traveler sees little of Nature that is revealed to the home-stayer. You will find she has made her home where you have made yours, and intimacy with her there becomes easy. Familiarity with things about one should not dull the edge of curiosity or interest. The walk you take today through the fields and woods, or along the river-bank, is the walk you should take tomorrow, and next day, and next. What you miss once, you will hit upon next time. The happenings are at intervals and are irregular. The play of Nature has no fixed programme. If she is not at home today, or is in a non-committal mood, call tomorrow, or next week. It is only when the wild creatures are at home, where their nests or dens are made, that their characteristics come out.

Field and Study (1919)

***

"Therefore am I still a lover
of the meadows and the woods, and mountains;
and of all that we behold from this green earth."
~William Wordsworth
"On Revisiting the Banks of the Wye,
July 13, 1798"

36
Tracks of the Eternal

My readers sometimes write me and complain that there is too much Nature in my books and not enough God, which seems to me like complaining that there is too much about the sunlight and not enough about the sun.

. . .

I look upon Nature not merely as the garment of God, but as his living integument [outer layer or skin]. With a [humanlike] God, the maker and ruler of the universe, and existing apart from it, I can do nothing.

When I write about Nature and make much of her beauties and wonders, I am writing about God. The Nature-lover is the God-lover. I am [cautious] about using the term "God" because of its theological and other disturbing associations.... But call it Nature and it is brought immeasurably near. I see it, touch it, hear it, smell it. I see the flowers, the birds, and all engaging aspects of field and wood and sky. I am a part of it. I see my absolute dependence upon it, and that denying it or slighting it, or turning my back upon it, [would be] like denying or slighting gravity.

Where are the tracks we made in the snow last winter? How real they seemed! How much they expressed! They told which way we were going, whether we were hurrying or sauntering, what we had on our feet, and they might easily tell if we bore a burden, or if we were drunk or sober, if we were man, or woman, or child. They were real. The snow still exists in the form of water or vapor, and the feet that imprinted themselves upon the snow may still exist, but the tracks that meant so much—where are they? The track was simply a record, like any other print or writing, and does not exist apart from the material substance that gave and took the impression. Are we ourselves anything more than the tracks of the Eternal in the dust of earth?

Field and Study (1919)

***

"Obviously such a path
could only be travelled by one
who was very alert and very sensitive
to the landmarks of a trackless wilderness."
~Thomas Merton
The Wisdom of the Desert

37
A Good Seasoning

In my excursions into nature, science plays a part, but not the leading part; it is like a silent monitor and friend who speaks when spoken to. Or I may say that I carry it in the back of my head and only now and then in the front. I do not go forth as an ornithologist taking note of the birds, nor as a botanist taking note of the flowers, nor as a zoologist studying the wild creatures, nor as a biologist, peeping and prying into the mysteries of life, but as a nature-lover pure and simple, who gathers much through sympathy and observation.

I am committed to no specific object; my walk is satisfactory if I fail to add a particle to my store of nature knowledge.

Oh, the wisdom that grows on trees, that murmurs in the streams, that floats in the wind, that sings in the birds, that is fragrant in the flowers, that speaks in the storms—the wisdom that one gathers on the shore, or when sauntering in the fields, or in resting under a tree, the wisdom that makes him forget his science, and exacts only his love—how precious it all is!

Love of nature does not depend upon exact knowledge, though exact knowledge has its value. My interest in the rocks, in the fields, and in the cliffs above them is enhanced by what science has told me about them, but is not summed up by that. A knowledge of the fundamentals of geology greatly adds to one's enjoyment of the earth's features. Science is always a good seasoning, but one does not want too much of a good seasoning.

Field and Study (1919)

***

> *"Relations are what matter most,*
> *and the health of the cultivated turns on*
> *the health of the wild."*
> ~Michael Pollan
> *The Omnivore's Dilemma*

38

A New Creed

Amid the decay of creeds, love of nature has high religious value.... It has made [naturalists] contented and at home wherever they are in nature—in the house not made with hands. This house is their church, and the rocks and the hills are the altars, and the creed is written in the leaves of the trees and in the flowers of the field and in the sands of the shore. A new creed every day and new preachers, and holy days all the week through. Every walk to the woods is a religious rite, every bath in the stream is a saving ordinance. Communion service is at all hours, and the bread and wine are from the heart and marrow of Mother Earth. There are no heretics in Nature's church; all are believers, all are communicants. The beauty of natural religion is that you have it all the time.... The crickets chirp it, the birds sing it, the breezes chant it, the thunder proclaims it, the streams murmur it.... Its incense rises from the plowed fields, it is on the morning breeze, it is in the forest breath and in the spray of the wave.... It is not even a faith; it is a love, an enthusiasm, a consecration to natural truth.

Accepting the Universe (1920)

***

"There is an excess in spiritual searching
that is profound ignorance.
Let that ignorance be our teacher!
...
A deep silence revives the listening
and the speaking of those two
who meet on the riverbank."
~Rumi
"Birdsong from Inside the Egg"
The Essential Rumi

39
At Home on this Planet

The old conception of an external God, the supreme ruler of the universe, with whom Moses talked and walked and even saw the hinder parts of, is out of date in our time. Still the overarching thought of the Infinite and the Eternal, in whom we live and move and have our being, must at times awaken in the minds of all of us, and lend dignity and sobriety to our lives.

But the other world fades as this world brightens. Science has made this world so interesting and wonderful, and our minds find such scope in it for the exercise of all their powers, that thoughts of another world are becoming foreign to us. We shall never exhaust the beauties and the wonders and the possibilities of this. To feel at home on this planet, and that it is, with all its drawbacks, the best possible world, I look upon as the supreme felicity of life.

When we look at it in its mere physical and chemical aspects, its play of forces, tangible and intangible, its reservoir of energy, its 'journeying of atoms,' its radiating electrons, its magnetic currents, its transmutations and cycles of change, its hidden but potent activities, its streaming auroras, its changing seasons, its myriad forms of life, and a thousand other things—all make it a unique and most desirable habitation.

Accepting the Universe (1920)

***

"He kept looking to the heavens
as if the answer were anywhere but here.
I was so bored with our goodness
I couldn't suck the juice
from one more pear.

It's here, I kept telling him,
here, rooted in the soil
like every other tree you know.
And I wove us a bed
of its uppermost branches."
~Alison Hawthorne Deming
from "Eve Revisited"
in *Science and Other Poems*

40
Land of Nowhere

Our religion is at fault, our saints have betrayed us, our theologians have blackened and defaced our earthly temple, and swapped it off for cloud mansions in the Land of Nowhere. The heavens embrace us always; the far-off is here, close at hand; the ground under your door-stone is a part of the morning star. If we could only pull ourselves up out of our absorption in trivial affairs, out of the petty turmoil of our practical lives, and see ourselves and our world in perspective and as a part of the celestial order, we could cease to weep and wail over our prosaic existence.

The astronomic view of our world, and the Darwinian view of our lives must go together. As one came out of the whirling, fiery nebulae, so the other came out of the struggling, slowly evolving, biological world of the unicellular life of the old seas.

Biologic time sets its seal upon one, and cosmic time upon the other. Dignity and beauty and meaning are given to our lives when we see far enough and wide enough, when we see the forces that minister to us, and the natural order of which we form a part.

Accepting the Universe (1920)

***

"Bending over the stone,
smelling earth up close,
we drank sky off the surface of water."
~Linda Hogan
Dwellings:
A Spiritual History of the Living World

41

Nature is a Great Traveler

The whole living world is so interrelated and interdependent, and hinges so completely upon the non-living, that our analysis and interpretation of it must of necessity be very imperfect. But the creative energy works to no specific ends, or rather it works to all ends. As every point on the surface of the globe is equally on the top at all times, so the whole system of living nature balances on any given object. I saw a book of poems recently, called 'The Road to Everywhere'—vague as Nature herself. All her roads are roads to everywhere. They may lead you to your own garden, or to the North Pole, or to the fixed stars, or may end where they began.

Nature is a great traveler, but she never gets away from home; she takes all her possessions along with her, and her course is without direction, and without beginning or end. The most startling contradiction you can make expresses her best. She is the sum of all opposites, the success of all failures, the good of all evil.

Accepting the Universe (1920)

***

"One of the sweet and expectable aspects
of life afloat is the perpetual present moment one lives in
and a perception that time is
nothing more than the current,
an eternal flowing back to the sea."
~William Least Heat-Moon
River-Horse: A Voyage Across America

42

On the Side of Life

On a midsummer day, calm, clear, warm, the leaves shining, the grain and grass ripening, the waters sparkling, the birds singing, we see and feel the beneficence of Nature. How good it all is! What a joy to be alive! If the day were to end in a fury of wind and storm, breaking the trees, unroofing the houses, and destroying the crops, we should be seeing the opposite side of Nature, what we call the malevolent side. Fair days now and then have such endings, but they are the exception; living nature survives them and soon forgets them. Their scars may long remain, but they finally disappear. Total nature is overpoweringly on the side of life. But for all this, when we talk bout the fatherhood of God, his loving solicitude, we talk in parables. There is not even the shadow of analogy between the wholesale bounty of Nature and the care and providence of a human father. Striding through the universe goes the Eternal, crushed worlds on one hand and worlds being created on the other; no special act of love or mercy or guidance, but a providence like the rains, the sunshine, the seasons.

When we say hard things about Nature—accuse her of cruelty, of savagery, of indifference—we fall short of our proper filial respect toward her. She is the mother of us all.

Accepting the Universe (1920)

***

"When the people call Earth 'Mother,'
they take with love
and with love give back
so that all may live."
~Marilou Awiakta
Seeking the Corn-Mother's Wisdom

43

The Marvelous Universe

Science tends more and more to reveal to us the unity that underlies the diversity of nature. We must have diversity in our practical lives; we must seize Nature by many handles. But our intellectual lives demand unity, demand simplicity amid all this complexity. Our religious lives demand the same. Amid all the diversity of creeds and sects we are coming more and more to see that religion is one, that verbal differences and ceremonies are unimportant, and that the fundamental agreements are alone significant. Religion as a key or passport to some other world has had its day; as a mere set of statements or dogmas about the Infinite mystery it has had its day. Science makes us more and more at home in this world, and is coming more and more, to the intuitional mind, to have a religious value. Science kills credulity and superstition, but to the well-balanced mind it enhances the feeling of wonder, of veneration, and of kinship which we feel in the presence of the marvelous universe. It quiets our fears and apprehensions, it pours oil upon the troubled waters of our lives, and reconciles us to the world as it is.

Accepting the Universe (1920)

***

"Surely I never had so clear an idea before
of the capacity to bless of mere Earth,
merely the beautiful Earth,
when fresh from the original breath
of the creative spirit."
~Margaret Fuller
Letter to Mary Rotch, January 21, 1844

44

Immortality

It is not you and I that are immortal; it is Creative Energy, of which we are a part. Our immortality is swallowed up in this.

The poets, the prophets, the martyrs, the heroes, the saints—where are they? Each was but a jewel in the dew, the rain, the snowflake—throbbing, burning, flashing with color for a brief time and then vanishing, adorning the world for a moment and then caught away into the great abyss. "O spendthrift Nature!" our hearts cry out; but Nature's spending is only the ceaseless merging of one form into another without diminution of her material or blurring of her types. Flowers bloom and flowers fade, the seasons come and the seasons go, men are born and men die, the world mourns for its saints and heroes, its poets and saviors, but Nature remains and is as young and spontaneous and inexhaustible as ever. Where is the comfort in all this to you and to me? There is none, save the comfort or satisfaction of knowing things as they are.... In the end each of us will have had his day, and can say as Whitman does,
"I have positively appeared. That is enough."

Accepting the Universe (1920)

***

"Wind goes from farm to farm in wave on wave,
But carries no cry of what is hoped to be.
There may be little or much beyond the grave,
But the strong are saying nothing until they see."
~Robert Frost
"The Strong Are Saying Nothing"

45
The Apple Leaf

As I sit here under an old heavy-topped apple-tree on a hot midsummer day, a yellow leaf lets go its hold upon the branch over my head and comes softly down upon the open book I am reading. It is a perfect leaf, but it has had its day. The huge family of leaves of which it was a member are still rank and green and active in sustaining the life of the tree, but this one has dropped out of the leafy ranks. There are a few small dark spots upon it, which, I see with my pocket glass, are fungus growths, or else some germ disease of apple-tree leaves, perhaps, like pneumonia, or diphtheria, or tuberculosis among men. One leaf out of ten thousand has fallen. Was Fate cruel to it? From the point of view of the leaf, yes—could a leaf have a point of view; from the point of view of Nature, no. The tree has leaves enough left to manufacture the needed chlorophyll, and that satisfies the law. If all the leaves were blighted, or were swept off by insect enemies, or stripped by hail and storm, that [would be] a calamity to the tree. But one leaf, though all the myriad forces of nature went to its production, though it is a marvel of delicate structure and function, though the sun's rays have beaten upon it and used it, and been kind to it, though evolution worked for untold ages to bring its kind to perfection—what matters it? It will go back into the soil and the air from which it came, and contribute its mite to another crop of leaves, and maybe it has rendered the molecules of carbon and hydrogen and oxygen of which it is composed more ready and willing to enter into other living combinations.... In the sum total of things, the life of this old tree counts for but little, but if it failed to bear apples, its chief end would be defeated.

Accepting the Universe (1920)

***

"This is what the Lord God showed me—
a basket of summer fruit.
The Lord said, 'Amos, what do you see?'
And I said, 'A basket of summer fruit.'"
~The Prophet Amos

46
The God We Touch

The only alternative [to atheism] I see is to conceive of God in terms of universal Nature—a nature God in whom we really live and move and have our being, with whom our relation is as intimate and constant as that of the babe in its mother's womb, or the apple upon the bough. This is the God that science and reason reveal to us—the God we touch with our hands, see with our eyes, hear with our ears, and from whom there is no escape—a God whom we serve and please by works and not by words, whose worship is deeds, and whose justification is in adjusting ourselves to his laws and availing ourselves of his bounty, a God who is indeed from everlasting to everlasting.

. . .

Naturalism does not see two immeasurable realities, God and Nature, it sees only one, that all is Nature or all is God, just as you prefer.... The universe was not made; it *is*, and always has been. God is Nature, and Nature is God.

. . .

Most persons are pantheists without knowing it. Ask any of the good orthodox folk what God is, and they will say that

he is a spirit. Ask them where he is, and they will answer,
He is here, there, everywhere, in you and in me. And this is
pantheism—all god—cosmotheism.

Accepting the Universe (1920)

***

"{My father} also taught me the earth was alive.
While I understood this with my mind,
my body had forgotten the startling physical evidence
of this living planet.
Perhaps I forgot because
it had been too long since
I'd put my hands on the Earth and listened."
~Brenda Peterson
Living By Water

47
Circles

Our astronomy is sound, but our actual life gives us no clue to its truths. Only when we turn philosophers do we know the tremendous voyage we are making, and then we only know it abstractly. We never can know it concretely. The swift turning of the planet under our feet, and its enormous speed in its orbit around the sun, are not revealed to our sense as motion, but as changes from night to day and from one season to another. Slow, soft, still, the moon and the sun rise and drift across the heavens, and the impassive earth seems like a ship becalmed. No hint at all of the more than rifle-bullet speed through space. It is all too big for us. The celestial machine is no machine at all to our sense, but its vast movements go on as gently and as easily as the falling of the dew or the blooming of the flowers, and almost as unconsciously to us as the circulation of the blood in our hearts.

We are in the heavens and are a part of the great astronomical whirl and procession, and know it not. It is symbolical of our lives generally. We do not realize that we are a part of Nature till we begin to think about it. Our lives proceed as if we were two—[humanity] and Nature—two great antagonistic or contrary facts, but the two are one; there is only Nature.

We can draw circle within circle, and circle around circle, but we cannot circumscribe Nature. That is the fact over all.

Accepting the Universe (1920)

***

"Tao is its own source and its own root.
It existed before heaven and earth and for all eternity.
It causes spirits and gods to be divine....
It was born before heaven and earth but not long ago....
No one knows her beginning
and no one knows her end."
~Chuang Tsu
Inner Chapters

48
In All the Flowing Currents

We create the world in which we live. I love Nature, but Nature does not love me. Love is an emotion which rocks and clouds do not feel. Nature loves me in my fellow beings. The breezes caress me, the morning refreshes me, the rain on the roof soothes me—that is, when I am in a mood to be caressed and refreshed and soothed. The main matter is the part I play in these things. All is directed to me and you because we are adjusted to all. No more is the kite or the sail adjusted to the wind, the water-wheel to the falling water, than are we adjusted to outward Nature. She is the primary and everlasting fact; we, as living beings, are the secondary and temporary facts.

. . .

I shall not be imprisoned in the grave where you are to bury my body. I shall be diffused in great Nature, in the soil, in the air, in the sunshine, in the hearts of those who love me, in all the living and flowing currents of the world, though I may never again in my entirety be embodied in a single human being.

My elements and my forces go back into the original sources out of which they came, and these sources are perennial in this vast, wonderful, divine cosmos.

Accepting the Universe (1920)

***

"I said, 'I will water my best garden,
and will water abundantly my garden bed':
and lo, my brook became a river,
and my river became a sea."
~Sirach

49
A Sense of Smell

How much is in a name! When we call the power back of all God, it smells of creeds and systems, of superstition, intolerance, persecution; but when we call it Nature, it smells of spring and summer, of green fields and blooming groves, of birds and flowers and sky and stars. I admit that it smells of tornadoes and earthquakes, of jungles and wildernesses, of disease and death, too, but these things make it all the more real to us.

The word "God" has so long stood for the conception of a being who sits apart from Nature, who shapes and rules it as its maker and governor. It is part of the conception of a dual or plural universe, God and Nature. This offends my sense of the oneness of creation. It seems to me that there is no other adequate solution of the total problem of life and Nature than what is called "pantheism," which identifies mind and matter, finite and Infinite, and sees in all these diverse manifestations one absolute being. As Emerson truly says, pantheism does not belittle God, it magnifies him. God becomes the one and only ultimate fact that fills the universe and from which we can no more be estranged than we can be estranged from gravitation.

. . .

As we cannot get away from Nature, we cannot get away from the Eternal. He sticketh closer than a brother, closer than the blood in our own hearts, not always to bless and to cheer, often to hinder and depress. Not all ease and joy is life; it is as often struggle, tears, defeat....

Not by placing God afar off in the heavens—a supersensuous, supermundane, supernatural being—do we make the problem easier.... When we see man as a part of Nature, we see him as a part of God.

Accepting the Universe (1920)

***

"A wild rhythm pulses in our blood.
A wild river pulses in our blood."
~Lorraine Anderson
"Wilderness in the Blood"
The Soul Unearthed

50
No Particle is Lost

Be assured that no particle of soul or body can be lost. But processes may cease; the flame of the lamp may go out, and the sum total of force and matter remain the same. When a blade of grass dies, a process has ended, and as mysterious a process as went on in Caesar's brain and body. And when all life on the earth and in our universe ceases, if it ever does, the problem would remain just as puzzling, if we can fancy ourselves still here to puzzle over it. We are links in an endless cycle of change in which we cannot separate the material from what we call the spiritual.

The water in our bodies today may have flashed as a dewdrop yesterday or lent itself to the splendor of the sunrise or sunset, or played a part in the bow in the clouds. Tomorrow it may be whirling in the vortex of a tornado, or helping to quench the life of a drowning man, or glistening in the frost figures on the window-pane. The movements of the brain molecules in which the phenomena of thought and consciousness are so mysteriously involved, they, too, are links in the cycle of change.

. . .

Each of us is an incarnation of the universal mind, as is every beast of the field and jungle, and every fowl of the air, and every insect that creeps and flies; and we can only look upon creation as an end in itself.... [Humanity] is a link in an endless chain of being.

Accepting the Universe (1920)

***

"Such deep coziness does not come quickly or easily, but anyone can begin to weave together the strands of the surrounding Earth into meaningful forms."
~Joseph Meeker
Minding the Earth

51
Heaven on Earth

Truly things are not what they seem. When we put heaven and earth far apart, we think as children. Heaven and earth are pretty close together. The shortest arm can reach from one to the other. When we go to heaven we shall not have far to travel, and I dare say the other place is quite as near, and, if reports be true, the road is broader and easier to travel. What children we are in such matters! The wisest men have the language of ignorance and superstition imposed upon them. How difficult it is not to think of the heavens up there as a reality, something above us and superior to us, a finer world, nearer God, lighted by the stars, the abode of spirits, the source of all good, our final celestial home....

In our floods of religious emotion we instinctively look away from the earth. The mystery, the immensity, the purity of the heavens above us make us turn our faces [upward], and as naturally make us turn downward when we consider the source of evil. The poor old earth which has mothered us and nursed us we treat with scant respect. Our awe and veneration we reserve for the worlds we know not of. Our senses sell us out.

The mud on our shoes disenchants us. It is only Whitman with his cosmic consciousness that can closely relate the heavens and the earth:

"Underneath the divine soil,
Overhead the sun."

Accepting the Universe (1920)

***

"Shall we not learn from life
its laws, dynamics, balances?
Learn to base our needs
not on death, destruction, waste,
but on renewal?
In wisdom and in gentleness learn
to walk again with Eden's angels?
Learn at last to shape a civilization
in harmony with the earth?"
~Nancy Newhall
This Is the American Earth

52
Upon This Rock

O nly a faith founded upon the rock of natural law can weather such a storm as the world passed through in [war], but unfortunately such a faith is possible to comparatively few.... Persons who do not read the book of nature as a whole, who do not try their faith by the records of the rocks and the everlasting stars, who are oblivious to the great law of evolution which has worked out the salvation of man and of all living things...those who take no account of all these things soon lose their reckoning in times like ours.

. . .

Our ecclesiastical faith must be housed in churches and kept warm by vestments. The moment we take it out into the open and expose it to unroofed and unwarmed universal nature, it is bound to suffer from the cosmic chill. For my part, I do not have to take my faith in out of the wet and the cold. It is an open-air faith, an all-the-year-round faith; neither killing frosts nor killing heats disturb it; not tornadoes nor earthquakes nor wars nor pestilence nor famine make me doubt for one moment that the universe is sound and good.... I do not mind if you call [the forces that brought us here and provide for us] material forces; the material and the spiritual are inseparable. I do not mind if you call this view the infidelity (or atheism) of science; science, too, is divine; all knowledge is knowledge of God.

I have never taken shelter in any form of ecclesiasticism.... I have inured my mind to the open air of the universe, to things as they are [always knowing] that the Creative Energy has our good at heart and always will have it.

Accepting the Universe (1920)

***

"I am still here, still flat on the hillside
hidden from the wind, but somehow I extend
above and beyond and around myself
to include the tree, the earth, the rocks, the breeze.
The earth, the rocks, the sky, and I interpenetrate.
We are one."
~Barbara Dean
Wellspring

53
More Than Beauty

The work of a genius is of a different order. Most current verse is merely sweetened prose put up in verse form. It serves its purpose; the mass of readers like it. Nearly all educated persons can turn it off with little effort....

...

There certainly can be no great poetry without a great philosopher behind it—a man who has thought and felt profoundly upon nature and upon life, as Wordsworth himself surely had. The true poet, like the philosopher, is a searcher after truth, and a searcher at the very heart of things—not cold, objective truth, but truth which is its own testimony, and which is carried alive into the heart by passion. He seeks more than beauty, he seeks the perennial source of beauty. The poet leads man to nature as a mother leads her child there—to instill a love of it into his heart. If a poet adds neither to my knowledge nor to my love, of what use is he?

...

When I say that every true poet must have a philosophy, I do not mean that he must be what is commonly called a philosophical poet; from such we steer clear. The philosophy in a poem must be like the iron in the blood. It is the iron that gives color and vigor to the blood. Reduce it and we become an anemic and feeble race. Much of the popular poetry is anemic in this respect. There is no virile thought in it. All of which amounts to saying that there is always a great nature back of a great poem.

The Last Harvest (1922)

***

"When the act of reflection takes place in the mind,
when we look at ourselves in the light of thought,
we discover that our life is embosomed in beauty."
~Ralph Waldo Emerson
"Spiritual Laws"

54
For My Having Lived

If the world is any better for my having lived in it, it is because I have pointed the way to a sane and happy life on terms within reach of all, in my love and joyous acceptance of the works of Nature about me. I have not tried, as the phrase is, to lead my readers from Nature up to Nature's God, because I cannot separate the one from the other. If your heart warms toward the visible creation, and toward your fellow human beings, you have the root of the matter in you. The power we call God does not sustain a mechanical or secondary relation to the universe, but is vital in it, or one with it. To give this power human {features} and attributes, as our parents did, only limits and belittles it. And to talk of leading from Nature up to Nature's God is to miss the God that throbs in every spear of grass and vibrates in the wing of every insect that hums. The Infinite is immanent in this universe.

. . .

There is no future for {Nature}, only an everlasting present. What is the very bloom and fragrance of humanity to the Infinite?

. . .

But what is the fruit of the flower of human life?.... The only fruit I can see is in fairer flowers, or a higher type of mind and life that follows in this world, and to which our lives may contribute.... You and I perish, but something goes out, or may go out, from us that will help forward a higher type of humanity.

The Last Harvest (1922)

***

"When you consider something like death, after which...
we may well go out like a candle flame,
then it probably doesn't matter if we try too hard,
are awkward sometimes, care for one another too deeply,
are excessively curious about nature,
are too open to experience, enjoy a nonstop expense of the senses
in an effort to know life intimately and lovingly."
~Diane Ackerman
A Natural History of the Senses

Editor's note: this fragment was among the very last things written by John Burroughs

55

The Fox and the Mitten

When I was about ten or twelve, a spell was put upon me by a red fox.... The baying of a hound upon the mountain had drawn me there, armed with the same old musket. It was a chilly day in early December. I took up my stand in the woods near what I thought might be the runway, and waited. After a while I stood the butt of my gun upon the ground, and held the barrel with my hand. Presently I heard a rustle in the leaves, and there came a superb fox loping along past me, not fifty feet away. He was evidently not aware of my presence, and, as for me, I was aware of his presence alone. I forgot that I had a gun, that here was the game I was in quest of, and that now was my chance to add to my store of silver quarters. As the unsuspecting fox disappeared over a knoll, again I came to my senses, and brought my gun to my shoulder; but it was too late, the game had gone. I returned home full of excitement at what I had seen, and gave as the excuse why I did not shoot, that I had my mitten on, and could not reach the trigger of my gun. It is true I had my mitten on, but there was a mitten, or something, on my wits also. It was years before I heard the last of that mitten; when I failed at anything they said, "John had his mitten on, I guess."

Our Friend John Burroughs (Clara Barrus, 1914)

***

*"Foxes have holes, and birds of the air have nests;
but {the real human being has}
nowhere to lay {their} head."*
~Jesus of Nazareth
Gospel of Matthew

56
Bone of My Bone

I am as fond of going forth for berries as my mother was, even to this day. Every June I must still make one or two excursions to distant fields for wild strawberries, or along the borders of the woods for black raspberries, and I never go without thinking of Mother. You could not see all that I bring home with me in my pail on such occasions; if you could, you would see the traces of daisies and buttercups and bobolinks, and the blue skies, with thoughts of Mother and the Old Home, that date from my youth. I usually eat some of the berries in bread and milk, as I was wont to do in the old days, and am, for the moment, as near a boy again as it is possible for me to be.

No doubt my life as a farm boy has had much to do with my subsequent love of nature, and my feeling of kinship with all rural things. I feel at home with them; they are bone of my bone and flesh of my flesh. It seems to me a man who was not born and reared in the country can hardly get Nature into his blood, and establish such intimate and affectionate relations with her, as can the born [countryperson]. We are so susceptible and so plastic in youth; we take things so seriously; they enter into and color and feed the very currents of our being. As a child I think I must have been more than usually fluid and impressionable, and that my affiliations with open-air life and objects were very hearty and thorough. As I grow old

I am experiencing what, I suppose, all men experience, more or less; my subsequent days slough off, or fade away, more and more, leaving only the days of my youth as a real and lasting possession.

Our Friend John Burroughs (Clara Barrus, 1914)

***

"But the God of my childhood
—that fierce old man in the sky—
was gone forever; dogma, theology—
all were gone, vanished, utterly refused by
my new understanding of the world....
I became sure that no existing belief system
would ever work for me in its entirety;
I would have to slowly, painfully,
twig by tiny twig, build my own spiritual home."
~Sharon Butala
"Living Inside the Landscape"
in *When the Wild Comes Leaping Up*
David Suzuki, editor

57
Sunday School

As a youth I never went to Sunday-school, and I was not often seen inside the church. My Sundays were spent rather roaming in the woods and fields, or climbing to "Old Clump," or, in summer, following the streams and swimming in the pools. Occasionally I went fishing, though this was to incur parental displeasure—unless I brought home some fine trout, in which case the displeasure was much tempered. I think this Sunday-school in the woods and fields was, in my case, best. It has always seemed, and still seems, as if I could be a little more intimate with Nature on Sunday than on a week-day; our relations were and are more ideal, a different spirit is abroad, the spirit of holiday and not of work, and I could in youth, and can now, abandon myself to the wild life about me more fully and more joyously on that day than on any other.

The memory of my youthful Sundays is fragrant with wintergreens, black birch, and crinkle-root, to say nothing of the harvest apples that grew in our neighbor's orchard; and the memory of Sundays in later years is fragrant with arbutus, and the showy orchid, and wild strawberries, and touched with the sanctity of woodland walks and hilltops. What day can compare with a Sunday to go to the waterfalls...? What sweet peace and repose is over all! The snakes...are as free from venom as are grasshoppers, and the grasshoppers themselves fiddle and dance as at no other time. Cherish your Sundays. I think you will read a little deeper in "Nature's infinite book of secrecy" on Sunday than on Monday.

Our Friend John Burroughs (Clara Barrus, 1914)

***

"Nature hath bound {God and Humanity}
by ties of kindred each to each."
~Epictetus
The Golden Sayings

58
Healthy Writing

The current of the lives of many persons, I think, is like a muddy stream. They lack the instinct for health, and hence do not know when the vital current is foul. They are never really well…. The dew on the grass, the bloom on the grape, the sheen on the plumage, are suggestions of the health that is within the reach of most of us.

The least cloud or film in my mental skies mars or stops my work. I write with my body quite as much as with my mind. How persons whose bread of life is heavy, so to speak—no lightness or buoyancy or airiness at all—can make good literature is a mystery to me…. I would live so that I could get tipsy on a glass of water, or find a spur in a whiff of morning air.

. . .

Life has been to me simply an opportunity to learn and enjoy, and, through my books, to share my enjoyment with others. I have thirsted to know things, and to make the most of them. The universe is to me a grand spectacle that fills me with awe and wonder and joy, and with intense curiosity…. I cannot, either in my writing or in my reading, tolerate any delay…any beating about the bush, even if there is a bird in it….

. . .

Those writers who are like stillwater fishermen, whose great virtues are patience and a tireless arm, never appealed to me any more than such fishing ever did. I want something more like a mountain brook—motion, variety, and the furthest possible remove from stagnation.

Indeed, where can you find a better symbol of good style in literature than a mountain brook...not too hurried, and not too loitering—limpid, musical, but not noisy, full but not turbid, sparkling but not frothy, every shallow quickly compensated for by a deep reach of thought; the calm, lucid pools of meaning alternating with the passages of rapid description, of moving eloquence or gay comment—flowing, caressing, battling, as the need may be, loitering at this point, hurrying at that, drawing together here, opening out there—freshness, variety, lucidity, power.

Our Friend John Burroughs (Clara Barrus, 1914)

***

*"But those of us who love smooth waters and quiet scenes,
can at least set before our fast countrymen and women
the dangers of haste, and the open and inviting fields
of health and recreation, where the overtasked and
broken down may regain in fresh and quiet pursuits,
that strength they have destroyed by their
over hasty living.... Let nature's breath breathe
into your failing lungs the healing of her own."*
~Elizabeth C. Wright
Lichen Tufts

59
The Simple Life

I am bound to praise the simple life, because I have lived it and found it good.... I love a small house, plain clothes, simple living. Many persons know the luxury of a skin bath—a plunge in the pool or the wave unhampered by clothing. That is the simple life—direct and immediate contact with things, life with the false wrappings torn away—the fine house, the fine equipage, the expensive habits, all cut off. How free one feels, how good the elements taste, how close one gets to them, how they fit one's body and one's soul! To see the fire that warms you, or better yet, to cut the wood that feeds the fire that warms you; to see the spring where the water bubbles up that slakes your thirst, and to dip your pail into it; to see the beams that are the stay of your four walls, and the timbers that uphold the roof that shelters you; to be in direct and personal contact with the sources of your material life; to want no extras, no shields; to find the universal elements enough; to find the air and the water exhilarating; to be refreshed by a morning walk or an evening saunter; to find a quest of wild berries more satisfying than a gift of tropic fruit; to be thrilled by the stars at night; to be elated over a bird's nest, or over a wild flower in spring—these are some of the rewards of the simple life.

"An Outlook Upon Life" quoted in Our Friend John Burroughs (Clara Barrus, 1914)

***

*"You like the feel {of living outdoors},
and you wait for that sudden sense
of romance everywhere
which is the touch of something
big and simple and beautiful.
It is always beyond the walls...."*
~Edna Brush Perkins
The White Heart of Mojave

60

In Love with the Earth

Think of this huge globe as a living corpuscle in the veins of the Infinite, gross and inert to our dull senses, but vibrating and responding to influences and forces that are too vast for us to take in. Behold it floating through a sea of energy like a mote in the air, or a corpuscle in the veins, as insignificant a part of the Whole as [a glob of blood is in] the human body, but under the spell of the Whole, and a vital part of the Whole.

. . .

The spaces between the stars in Orion's belt, or in the Pleiades, would open to hundreds of millions of miles, if we could approach them. Like fruit on the same vine seem many groups of stars, but the spaces that really separate them overwhelm the mind that tries to grasp their magnitude. Ground-room is cheap in heaven; there are oceans of it to spare. The grouping of celestial bodies which we see are as of a flock of birds upon the same branch.

I never tire of contemplating the earth as it swims through space. As I near the time when I know these contemplations must cease, it is more and more in my thoughts—its beauty, its wonder, its meaning, and the grandeur of the voyage we are making on its surface. The imaginary and hoped-for other world occupies my thoughts very little. There is so much to know here, so much to enjoy, so much to engage every faculty of the mind and develop every power of the body, such beauty, such sublimity, and such a veil of enchantment and mystery over all—how can one ever tire of it, or wish for a better? I am in love with the earth. With all its hostile forces and forbidding features—its deserts, its jungles, its killing heats and frigid zones, its storms and earthquakes, its wars, and famines, and contagious diseases—I am thankful that my lot was not cast on any other planet. It is the best possible world, undoubtedly, for such beings as we are, and is slowly becoming better adapted to human life—ripening on the vast...tree whose fruit is worlds and systems.

Field and Study (1919)

***

"One of the reasons for wild places
is so other people can fall in love with them—
because surely there are others wired like me,
for whom this landscape will be enough."
~Bill McKibben
Wandering Home

***

"Waiting"

Serene, I fold my hands and wait,
   Nor care for wind, nor tide, nor sea;
I rave no more 'gainst Time or Fate,
   For lo! my own shall come to me.

I stay my haste, I make delays,
   For what avails this eager pace?
I stand amid the eternal ways,
   And what is mine shall know my face.

Asleep, awake, by night or day,
   The friends I seek are seeking me;
No wind can drive my bark astray,
   Nor change the tide of destiny.

What matter if I stand alone?
   I wait with joy the coming years;
My heart shall reap where it hath sown,
   And garner up its fruit of tears.

The waters know their own, and draw
    The brook that springs in yonder heights;
So flows the good with equal law
    Unto the soul of pure delights.

The stars come nightly to the sky;
    The tidal wave comes to the sea;
Nor time, nor space, nor deep, nor high,
    Can keep my own away from me.

The Light of Day (1904)

SOURCES

Works by John Burroughs

John Burroughs. *Accepting the Universe.* Boston: Houghton, Mifflin Company, 1920.

John Burroughs. *Field and Study.* The Writings of John Burroughs, Part Twenty. Boston: Houghton, Mifflin Company, 1919.

John Burroughs. *Locusts and Wild Honey.* The Writings of John Burroughs. Boston: Houghton, Mifflin and Company, 1904.

John Burroughs. *The Breath of Life.* The Writings of John Burroughs, Part Eighteen. Boston: Houghton, Mifflin Company, 1915.

John Burroughs. *The Last Harvest.* The Complete Writings of John Burroughs. N.Y.: William Wise and Company, 1924.

John Burroughs. *The Light of Day.* The Writings of John Burroughs, Vol. XVII. Boston: Houghton, Mifflin Company, 1904.

John Burroughs. *Wake-Robin.* Boston: Houghton, Mifflin and Company, 1902.

John Burroughs. *Ways of Nature.* The Writings of John Burroughs. Boston: Houghton, Mifflin and Company, 1905.

Works about John Burroughs

Clara Barrus. *Our Friend John Burroughs.* Amsterdam: Fredonia Books, 2001 (reprint of 1914 edition).

Edward Kanze. *The World of John Burroughs.* SF: Sierra Club Books, 1996.

Other Sources

John Muir: His Life and Letters and Other Writings. Terry Gifford, editor. Seattle: The Mountaineers, 1996.

Sisters of the Earth: Women's Prose and Poetry about Nature. Lorraine Anderson, editor. N.Y.: Vintage Books, 2003.

Tim Mallory. *The Catskill Archive* (online resource).

PHOTO CREDITS

Photographs © Chris Highland

Cover: Path of Light, South Whidbey State Park, Washington

Introduction: Universal web, Whidbey Island, Washington

Selection 1:   Leaf after autumn rain, Snohomish, Washington

Selection 10:   Bear Valley Creek, Point Reyes, California

Selection 20:   Kelpball, Whidbey Island, Washington

Selection 30:   Ravens & Salmon, Lake Washington, Seattle, Washington

Selection 40:   Driftwood beach, Whidbey Island, Washington

Selection 50:   Sky over Olympic Mountains, Washington

Selection 60:   Late afternoon, Lone Lake, Whidbey Island, Washington

Backcover: Winterfall. Marin Watershed, California

Photograph by Heather Voss

Author page: Chris by the Stilliguamish River,
                Washington

Library of Congress

Frontispiece: John Burroughs (1921)
                —one of his last portraits

Chris Highland, a native of western Washington State, has been a teacher, counselor, social worker and chaplain. He returned to the Pacific Northwest in 2005 after twenty-six years in the San Francisco Bay area. For a majority of those years he was an interfaith chaplain with homesearching ("homeless") people, jail detainees ("offenders") and those with exceptional physical and mental abilities (people with "disabilities").

He earned a Bachelor degree in Philosophy and Religion from Seattle Pacific University and a Master degree from San

Francisco Theological Seminary. For fourteen years he was an ordained Protestant minister before leaving to head upstream. He has taught courses and given presentations on spirituality and wisdom in churches, synagogues, temples and retreat centers.

Chris is the author of six books on natural spirituality including **Meditations of John Muir; Meditations of Henry David Thoreau; Meditations of Ralph Waldo Emerson; Meditations of Walt Whitman** (Wilderness Press), followed by **Meditations of Margaret Fuller** and **Meditations of John Burroughs.** Portions of his novel **Wild Teachers,** his stories of chaplaincy **My Address is a River,** his poetry **Edge of the Falls** and his forthcoming spiritual autobiography **Life** *After* **Faith** are published on his website at www.naturetemple.net along with numerous essays and photographs.

He currently lives on an island in the Puget Sound.

Made in the USA
Monee, IL
27 January 2023